Great
Moments in
OLYMPIC
SPORTS

SKIING

By Brian Trusdell

SportsZone

An Imprint of Abdo Publishing
www.abdopublishing.com

www.abdopublishing.com

Published by Abdo Publishing, a division of ABDO, PO Box 398166, Minneapolis, Minnesota 55439. Copyright © 2015 by Abdo Consulting Group, Inc. International copyrights reserved in all countries. No part of this book may be reproduced in any form without written permission from the publisher. SportsZone™ is a trademark and logo of Abdo Publishing.

Printed in the United States of America, North Mankato, Minnesota
042014
092014

THIS BOOK CONTAINS
RECYCLED MATERIALS

Cover Photo: Sergei Grits/AP Images
Interior Photos: Sergei Grits/AP Images, 1; Horst Faas/AP Images, 6–7; Stewart Fraser/Colorsport/Corbis, 9; Strumpf/AP Images, 13; Dieter Endlicher/AP Images, 14–15; PCN/Corbis, 17, 36–37; Armando Trovati/AP Images, 18; AP Images, 21; Diether Endlicher/AP Images, 22–23, 41; Luca Bruno/AP Images, 25; Jerome Prevost/TempSport/Corbis, 29; Jean-Yves Ruszniewski/TempSport/Corbis, 30–31; Alexander Zemlianichenko/AP Images, 35; Rudi Blaha/AP Images, 42; Matthias Schrader/AP Images, 44–45; Dmitry Lovetsky/AP Images, 48; Elaine Thompson/AP Images, 51; Mike Egerton/Press Association via AP Images, 52–53; Gero Breloer/AP Images, 57; Andy Wong/AP Images, 59

Editor: Chrös McDougall
Series Designer: Craig Hinton

Library of Congress Control Number: 2014932871

Cataloging-in-Publication Data
Trusdell, Brian.
 Great moments in Olympic skiing / Brian Trusdell.
   p. cm. -- (Great moments in Olympic sports)
Includes bibliographical references and index.
ISBN 978-1-62403-397-1
1. Downhill skiing--Juvenile literature.   2. Freestyle skiing--Juvenile literature.   3. Winter Olympics--Juvenile literature.   I. Title.
796.9--dc23

2014932871

Contents

Introduction

Winter Olympic sports must involve either ice or snow. Skiing events have been in every Olympic Winter Games since the first one, in 1924. Only Nordic skiing events were held until 1936. Alpine skiing was added to the Winter Games in 1936. Women's skiers joined the Olympics in 1936 (Alpine) and 1952 (Nordic).

Nordic skiing takes its name for the Nordic people of Scandinavia. They have long used skis as a mode of travel. Nordic has two major categories. One is cross-country skiing. These skiers race across generally flat land. Nordic skiing also includes ski jumping. The Nordic combined involves both ski jumping and a cross-country race.

Alpine skiing takes its name from the famous mountains in Central Europe, the Alps. These skiers race to get down a hill as fast as possible while navigating gates. The events are the slalom, giant slalom, super-giant slalom (super-G), and downhill. A fifth event, the super combined, involves a downhill and a slalom race.

Freestyle skiing is newer. It debuted in the Winter Games in 1992. These events involve some combination of style, tricks, speed, or all three. Five freestyle events were held in the 2014 Olympics. They were aerials, halfpipe, moguls, ski cross, and slopestyle.

1

Innsbruck 1976
A WILD RIDE

From the start house, a person could see the Alpine town of Innsbruck, Austria, in the distance. It looked like a perfect miniature model train platform that someone had spent years building. But Franz Klammer was instead staring at nearly two miles of a white, icy ski slope. The downhill is Alpine skiing's fastest race. Skiers reach speeds as fast as 80 miles per hour (129 km/h) wearing only a helmet, goggles, and a skintight body suit. And the downhill course at the 1976 Olympic Winter Games was harder than most. In fact, some said it was

The 1976 Olympic Winter Games were held in the picturesque town of Innsbruck, Austria.

too dangerous. The difficult course was not the only pressure Klammer faced, though. He was racing in his home country. And Austrians are among the most passionate Alpine skiing fans in the world.

To claim a gold medal would be difficult. Switzerland's Bernhard Russi had won the downhill race four years earlier at the Winter Games in Sapporo, Japan. He was the third skier on the hill in 1976. Russi had recorded an impressive time of 1 minute, 46.06 seconds. That was the mark Klammer would have to beat to win gold.

The final group had 15 skiers. Klammer was last. That meant he had to wait for each of his competitors. And nobody was coming close to Russi's time. Herbert Plank of Italy was the closest. But the best he could do was more than half a second behind.

Klammer hadn't done very well in practice runs earlier in the week. Hope was fading that he would win. But that didn't stop 60,000 people from lining the course.

Normally, Klammer ignored the other skiers' times. In his mind, he skied against the course, not the man. He just tried to ski as fast as he possibly could. But on this day, he couldn't ignore Russi. Loudspeakers were everywhere. The public address announcer praised Russi's run for all to hear.

"One moment I was thinking, 'How can I beat this guy [when] nobody else is getting anywhere near his time?'" Klammer said. "The next moment, I thought I could win."

Leaving It on the Hill

Klammer pushed out of the starting gate and immediately crouched into a tuck position. Nine seconds later, he was in trouble. As he leaned into a right-hand turn, he began to lose his balance. He was dangerously skiing on one foot as his left leg came up to keep him from falling. Former US Ski Team coach Bob Beattie was calling the race for ABC television. He noticed the problem right away.

"Trouble by Klammer right at the top. . . . He's right on the edge!" Beattie exclaimed.

An American First

Bill Johnson won the downhill at the 1984 Winter Games in Sarajevo, Yugoslavia. That made him the first American to win an Olympic gold medal in Alpine skiing. Johnson had claimed a World Cup victory on the famous Lauberhorn downhill course in Switzerland a month earlier. Then he had several good practice runs on the Olympic course. He boldly predicted victory, much to the annoyance of many of his European counterparts. But Johnson won with the fastest average speed in Olympic downhill history, reaching 64.95 mph (104.53 km/h) in completing the course.

By the first intermediate mark, Klammer trailed Russi by two-hundredths of a second, 32.24 seconds to 32.22. As he came upon the second big right-hand turn, Klammer appeared out of control. He came off a jump and looked ready to crash. His left arm reached straight up. His right arm shot straight out while his legs stretched to reach the snow.

"Klammer almost went down!" Beattie screamed.

By the second intermediate mark, Klammer had fallen further behind Russi. He was 19-hundredths of a second back. He needed to pick up speed. Klammer flew over jumps with nothing to lose. But as he turned again to his right, his momentum pushed him to the left edge of the course. He came within a few feet of the netting that held fans back.

Only a few hundred meters remained. Klammer ignored all caution. The final right turn was hard for skiers to see around the corner. Immediately after was a difficult little drop. Klammer made the turn. But he had too much speed while going over the drop. He came off the jump high. The wind pushed him out of his tuck and upright. His ski tips came up. But the backs of his skis touched and the tips slapped the snow. A wispy trail of dust blew up behind them.

Klammer tucked once more. There was one last drop right before the finish. But he again had to adjust to not crash. His right leg came up and quickly shot back down again before he crossed the finish line in 1:45.73. It was 33-hundredths of a second faster than Russi.

Klammer was an Olympic champion. As he slowed in the finish area, he glanced at the scoreboard to see his time. He thrust both arms in the air as he was drowned in cheers.

Russi was in the finish area awaiting the final results. He was the first to congratulate the man who would become known as "Kaiser" (Emperor) to his countrymen and "The Klammer Express" around the world.

Klammer had an impressive career. The World Cup is the top circuit of ski racing. Klammer won 26 World Cup races in his 12-year career. He also won five World Cup downhill titles and a world championship in the downhill. But he would be best known for that one day in 1976. Many consider it to be one of the most exciting Alpine skiing races of all time.

Two for Tommy Moe

Tommy Moe won both the super-G and combined races at the World Junior Ski Championships in 1989. But he had never won a World Cup race heading into the 1994 Winter Games in Lillehammer, Norway. The downhill was first. Moe beat out local favorite Kjetil Andre Aamodt by four-hundredths of a second to claim gold. Then Moe finished second in the super-G four days later. Again, he was just ahead of Aamodt. It was the first time an American man earned two medals in Alpine skiing in the same Olympic Winter Games.

Police help Austrian Franz Klammer move through an enthusiastic home crowd after his downhill victory at the 1976 Olympics.

2

Calgary 1988
IT'S TOMBA TIME

Alpine skiing fans were accustomed to skiers such as Ingemar Stenmark. Many considered him to be the greatest skier who ever lived. And Stenmark was known to be a gentleman and humble.

The World Cup ski circuit rarely had seen a character quite like Alberto Tomba. The 21-year-old Italian came into the 1988 Olympic Winter Games in Calgary, Canada, with a reputation, both good and bad. He was handsome, charming, and confident. Plus, he was on a roll. Tomba had never won a major race until two and a

Italy's Alberto Tomba races down the hill during the slalom at the 1988 Olympic Winter Games in Calgary, Canada.

half months before the Olympics. He then won seven of the 10 World Cup races he entered. His popularity exploded.

In Tomba's native Italy, television ratings for World Cup events quadrupled. Fans loved the man nicknamed "La Bomba" (Italian for "The Bomb"). Going into the Olympics, Tomba was a medal favorite in the slalom and giant slalom.

But Tomba also had other nicknames. After winning a race in Sestriere, Italy, he declared, "I am a beast." Soon some people began calling him "The Beast," though some used the nickname mockingly. That was because many saw Tomba as brash and arrogant.

Many Alpine skiers only compete in their specialty. The downhill and super-G are considered speed races. The slalom and giant slalom

Ingemar Stenmark

Ingemar Stenmark had won a record 13 World Cup races during the 1978–79 ski season. In September 1979, he was practicing the downhill. The 23-year-old Swede crashed and tumbled 200 yards (183 m) down the slope. He was knocked unconscious. His body shook with spasms. He foamed at the mouth. Five months later, Stenmark went to the 1980 Olympics in Lake Placid, New York. There he won both the giant slalom and, three days later, the slalom. Stenmark would go on to win 86 World Cup races—a record that still has not been approached—and become the most successful skier in history.

Alberto Tomba speeds down the Olympic giant slalom course in 1988.

are technical races. They feature more turns and less speed. Tomba was a technical skier. He was also good in the downhill and super-G. But he did not ski in those events because his mother thought they were too dangerous.

Tomba partially earned his "La Bomba" nickname from his skiing style. The gates in his era were not as flexible as those of today. So while most skiers clipped the gates in the slalom and giant slalom, Tomba barreled through them. At 6 feet 1 and 195 pounds, he was built like a typical

Alberto Tomba turns around a gate during the giant slalom at the 1988 Olympic Winter Games.

downhill skier. However, he had the agility of a slalom specialist. He skied very close to the gate poles. He often struck them with his shoulder, hips, and legs. Many times, course workers had to go back and reset them in the ground because Tomba knocked them out.

This style gave Tomba an advantage. He was able to ski a straighter line and maintain the downhill momentum. That translated into more speed and a faster time.

Going for It

Tomba's best event was the slalom. However, the giant slalom was scheduled first in Calgary. Before the race, Tomba wished his fellow competitors good luck. He then went out and skied the fastest time by 1.14 seconds. It gave him a huge lead. Austria's Hubert Strolz came in second. The race still had a second run, however. The two times would be added together to determine a winner.

Tomba skied a strong second run. Strolz was a tenth of a second faster. But since Tomba had such a big lead after the first run, he still won the race by 1.04 seconds.

Tomba's father was a wealthy textile merchant. He had promised his son that he would buy him a new Ferrari sports car if he won a gold medal. Talking to reporters after the race, Tomba told them: "I want it red."

But Tomba wasn't done. Two days later, Tomba skied in the slalom. This one wasn't as easy. He drew the eleventh starting position in the first run. The snow was melting as Tomba skied to the third-best time. He was 63-hundredths of a second behind Germany's Frank Woerndl and 18-hundredths behind Sweden's Jonas Nilsson. Again, however, he had one more run.

By the second run, new snow was falling. It made the course faster as the race went on. With the third-best time, Tomba skied third to last. He took as much time as he could at the start. Then he flung himself down the slope. He skied a second run of 47.85 seconds and took the lead.

But he had to watch as Nilsson and Woerndl came down. Nilsson was nearly a second worse than Tomba at 48.79 seconds. Tomba remained in first. Then Woerndl came down. But he couldn't come close to Tomba either. His time of 48.54 handed "La Bomba" his second gold medal.

Tomba was so confident that he felt the world was his. He was one of the biggest stars of the 1988 Winter Games. The other big star was East German figure skater Katarina Witt. East Germany was mostly closed off to the West at the time. Witt was by far the most famous East German athlete to westerners. So Tomba went to the women's figure skating finals

The Mahre Brothers

American Phil Mahre was the three-time defending World Cup overall champion when he arrived at the 1984 Winter Games in Sarajevo, Yugoslavia. But at 26, he and his twin brother, Steve, were nearing the end of their careers. And they did poorly in the giant slalom. Phil was eighth and Steve was seventeenth. The brothers acted as though it was not that important. US sportswriters criticized them bitterly. Five days later, in the slalom, Phil finished 21-hundredths of a second ahead of Steve to give the United States, and the Mahre brothers, a 1-2 finish.

Alberto Tomba celebrates after winning the giant slalom at the 1988 Olympic Winter Games.

to meet her. In the athletes' area, Tomba wore his two gold medals around his neck. He went up to ask Witt out for a date. He told her that he, too, was a gold medalist. She did not recognize him and asked him in which sport he won his medals.

"It was like shooting him with a gun," Witt said.

Tomba got the gold but not the girl.

3

Nagano 1998
CRASH COURSE

Like many Austrians, Hermann Maier started skiing at an early age. He was only six. And as he got older, many thought he had the ability to be one of his country's next stars. That was a big deal in a country where skiers are treated like football or baseball players are in America.

In his early teens, Maier hit a growth spurt. However, he suffered from Osgood-Schlatter disease, which weakened his knees. By 15, he had to quit racing at a high level. Maier spent the next seven winters working

Hermann Maier was one of Austria's best hopes for a gold medal at the 1998 Olympic Winter Games in Nagano, Japan.

as an instructor at his parents' ski school. In the summer, he worked as a bricklayer. But Maier continued racing at a semi-pro level. And by 1995, Austrian ski officials put him in the national ski program.

Within two years, Maier was skiing on the World Cup circuit. By the 1998 Olympic Winter Games, he had won 10 World Cup races. Fans called him "Das Monster." That is German for "The Monster." Another nickname was "The Herminator." That was a reference to the Terminator movies that were popular at the time. Austrian actor Arnold Schwarzenegger played the title cyborg character in the movies.

The 1998 Olympics were in Nagano, Japan. Maier was the favorite in the downhill, the super-G, and the giant slalom.

The Nagano downhill had many problems. First of all, many of the top skiers complained the hill was too short. Local officials made the course slightly longer. But they didn't make it as long as the skiers wanted. The officials wanted to avoid creeping into a national park.

Then there was the weather. Fog, snow, rain, and strong winds disrupted the racing. The downhill had to be delayed three times over five days. More wind on race day caused another 50-minute delay. The wind also forced officials to make an early jump smaller. To do that, Gate 7 was moved a few yards to the inside. But the change actually made the course

Hermann Maier gets big air during a training run for the downhill at the 1998 Olympic Winter Games.

faster. Plus, the temperature was higher than 50 degrees, so the hill was extra icy.

Maier skied fourth in the field of 43, right after Jean-Luc Cretier of France. Cretier took a cautious approach. He set the time that would eventually win the race. Maier didn't do anything cautiously.

He pushed powerfully out of the start house and quickly gained speed. Only 500 yards (457 m) down the slope, he came upon Gate 7.

Maier was just 18 seconds into his run. He was leaning into a right-hand turn with a left turn right after that.

Then the edge of his left ski got caught in the snow. His right leg came up and the rest of his body followed. Maier went airborne and sideways. Estimates were that he was traveling anywhere from 70–90 mph (113–145 km/h). Maier flipped upside down as he flew through the air, landing on his helmet. He came down on his right shoulder. His skis flew off. Then he cartwheeled another 50 yards (46 m), end over end. One sportswriter described Maier as looking "like a side of beef that had been tossed from a helicopter."

A Mysterious Helper

Austria's Toni Sailer won all three Alpine skiing gold medals at the 1956 Olympics. France's Jean-Claude Killy matched that feat at the 1968 Winter Games. But Killy's last medal in the slalom was controversial. His chief competitor was Karl Schranz of Austria. Schranz was skiing his second run when he said a mysterious person appeared on the course. The skier skidded to a halt and asked for a rerun. Three witnesses verified Schranz's claim. Officials granted him a rerun. When Schranz re-skied the course, he had the best time and won. But hours later, race officials said Schranz had missed two gates before seeing the mysterious figure. Schranz was disqualified. A race jury, with two French judges, upheld the ruling 3–1 and gave Killy his third gold.

Fences were set up to stop skiers from sliding off the course. But Maier crashed over one fence, then a second, and kept on going. He rolled over a small cliff before coming to a stop face down in the snow.

Some who watched the crash thought they had just seen a man die. They described it as horrific and scary. But slowly Maier crawled to his knees and cleared the snow from his goggles. He paused and bent back down as he tried to clear his head.

He finally got to his feet. Maier waved to the television camera to let his mother back in Austria know he was OK. A French skier had died four months earlier after colliding with her coach during practice. Soon after, Maier crashed at a race in Switzerland and didn't wave, causing his mother to panic.

Maier was able to walk away without help, but he was far from uninjured. Some thought his career might be over. Maier was hoping his Olympics weren't over. After all, the super-G was scheduled for the next day.

Amazing Comeback

Maier woke up the next morning so sore he couldn't walk. But rain caused the super-G to be postponed. The next day, fog forced another delay. Other skiers and fans complained about the delays. But Maier was thankful. Slowly, each day he got better. He was able to walk and move his shoulder and arms without pain.

By the third day, he was well enough to get back on the mountain. While some thought he would never ski again, Maier went out and won the super-G. He finished in 1 minute, 34.82 seconds. No other skier broke 1:35. The second-place finisher was more than a half of a second behind Maier at 1:35.43.

Three days after the super-G, and less than a week after his downhill crash, Maier won the giant slalom. He had the fastest time in both runs to win in 2:38.51. That was more than eight-tenths of a second ahead of silver medalist Stephan Eberharter of Austria. His time was 2:39.36.

Maier went on to win 13 World Cup races in the 1997–98 season. He also won the first of four World Cup overall titles. All of his

Kjetil Andre Aamodt

Kjetil Andre Aamodt already had won numerous honors by 2003. He had three Olympic gold medals, four World Championships medals, and several World Cup titles. But in October of that year while practicing, he crashed, breaking his ankle and tearing ligaments. The Norwegian missed the entire ski season. He didn't win another race until the 2006 Olympics in Turin, Italy, where he won the super-G for a third time. At 34, he became the only man to win four gold medals in Alpine skiing. It was his last major ski race victory.

accomplishments came after one of the most spectacular crashes in Olympic history. It is still shown today to demonstrate the extreme danger of downhill skiing.

Nagano 1998
HIGH FLYING

It was already the fifth day of the 1998 Olympic Winter Games in Nagano, Japan, and the United States still had not won a medal. That fact was somewhat embarrassing for Team USA. The Winter Games began in 1924. Since then, only Norway had won more medals than the United States. And US Olympic officials had predicted that the American team would have one of its best Olympic performances in Nagano.

US fans were starting to get antsy. Their best hope at the moment was a moguls skier named Jonny Moseley.

US skier Jonny Moseley performs a jump during the moguls event at the 1998 Olympic Winter Games in Nagano, Japan.

Moseley was a 22-year-old born in Puerto Rico. He didn't even see snow until he was three years old. Yet Moseley wasn't a long shot. He had won the overall Freestyle World Cup in both 1995 and 1996. Plus, he had won three of the six World Cup events in the two months before the Winter Games. However, he finished fifty-first in one of the other three.

But that was the nature of moguls. The event can be unpredictable. The run is about 200–300 yards (183–274 m) long. Large bumps, or moguls, fill most of the course. Plus, skiers also have to go off two large ramps and perform tricks. Twenty-five percent of the score is how fast they complete the course. The other 75 percent comes from judges'

Manic Moguls

No moguls skier has ever defended an Olympic gold medal. Vermont native Hannah Kearney learned that the hard way in the unpredictable event. She was the reigning world champion when she arrived at the 2006 Olympics. But she stumbled on a landing during her first jump in qualifying and didn't make the final round. Kearney returned to the Olympics in 2010 as the reigning World Cup champion. This time, she didn't disappoint. She finished first in qualifying. Then, skiing last in the medal portion of the competition, she had a clean run to clinch the gold medal. Once again, Kearney went into the 2014 Olympics as the favorite. This time she was the defending world and World Cup overall champ. However, a bobble on the upper moguls left her in third place behind Canadian sisters Chloe and Justine Dufour-Lapointe.

scores. They score the skiers on how well they get around the moguls (50 percent) and how well they perform tricks (25 percent).

Moseley already was in good position. He had the best qualifying score two days earlier when the field was cut to 16. Now the skiers were going in reverse order of finish. That meant he would go last.

Time to Shine

Moseley's chief competitor was Canada's Jean-Luc Brassard. Brassard was the defending Olympic champion. He had also won two World Cup events earlier in the season. But the Canadian had scored only 25.52 points in the final. Finland's Janne Lahtela (26.00) and Sami Mustonen (25.76) were ahead of him in the standings.

Moseley pushed off the edge of the hill at the start and began bouncing down Mount Iizuna. A large and energetic crowd waited at the bottom of the hill. His mom and dad were there chanting "U-S-A, U-S-A." Other fans rang bells and honked horns.

About one-third of the way down, he hit the first jump. He performed a double-twisting spread. That was a trick in which he twisted his hips back and forth twice and then spread his skis out before landing.

Then it was back to getting around moguls. Two-thirds of the way down was his big jump. Over the previous couple of years, Moseley had worked on a trick called a 360 Mute Grab. It was mostly for promotional films and fun. Some called it a "Helicopter" or an "Iron Cross" or a "Helicopter Iron Cross." That's because Moseley crossed his skis to make them look like the blades of a chopper or a cross. He then spun 360 degrees—a full turn. Moseley added a unique touch by pulling his legs up and grabbing the binding of his left ski with his right hand as he spun.

When he approached the jump, his lips tightened into a circle. Moseley took a breath through the small hole. Taking off, he got good air. Moseley then executed the jump flawlessly and landed with no problem.

The last thing he had to do was get to the bottom of the hill without falling. It took only 25 seconds to get from the beginning to the end. And when he crossed the finish line, Moseley knew he had won.

He thrust his arms up as he crossed under the finish banner, sprayed snow as he skidded to a stop, and then fell over into the pads surrounding the finish area. He got back up and again his arms went up in the air. He leaned back and looked into the bright beaming sun with his mouth wide open.

"I got number one!" Moseley yelled. "I can't believe it. Oh, my God. Now what do I do? I'm going to Disneyland . . . How about that? This is unbelievable. I never thought it would happen."

Jonny Moseley shows off his gold medal after winning the freestyle moguls event at the 1998 Olympic Winter Games.

When the scores were posted, Moseley was awarded 26.93, nearly a full point better than Lahtela. His run had been the second fastest of the day. But more important, his signature trick would become a staple of moguls skiers for years to come.

5

Nagano 1998
AN AMAZING COMEBACK

Picabo Street was such a daredevil as a kid that her mother shuddered when she went out to play. She'd "ski jump" off the chair lift from 20 feet (6.1 m) in the air. She'd wage BB gun wars with the boys in her town in an abandoned hotel. She'd play tackle football. She'd race BMX bikes. She'd box.

"My job was to keep her older brother fed and to keep Picabo alive," her mother said half-jokingly.

It was that daring nature that led Street to the downhill, skiing's fastest and most dangerous race.

US skier Picabo Street flies over a jump during the super-G at the 1998 Olympic Winter Games in Nagano, Japan.

Street won World Cup downhill titles in 1995 and 1996. She became the first American to win the World Cup downhill championship.

Her devil-may-care attitude also resulted in a lot of bruises and scrapes. But none were worse than those suffered in December 1996. Street crashed while training in Vail, Colorado. She was left with a broken bone in her left thigh and a torn anterior cruciate ligament in her left knee.

The injury came 14 months before the start of the 1998 Olympic Winter Games in Nagano, Japan. Street had earned the silver in the downhill at the 1994 Games in Lillehammer, Norway. She stood on the podium next to champion Katja Seizinger of Germany as the German national anthem played. It was then that Street vowed to win the next gold medal. Now that dream was in danger. She had a little more than a year to get back to world-class form. It was impossible for most. But Street was not like most.

Unique Name

Street was born in 1971 and grew up in Triumph, Idaho. Her parents Roland, also known as "Stubby," and Dee were hippies. That term describes people who reject many values considered normal in mainstream society. One value they rejected was in selecting their daughter's name. Street's parents listed her name as "Baby Girl" Street on her birth certificate. They planned to let her pick her own name when she got older.

The decision came sooner than expected. When Street was two, the family decided to take an overseas trip. To go, she needed a first name for her passport. So Stubby picked one. He knew his daughter loved playing the game "peek-a-boo." There was also a nearby town called Picabo. That name means "shining waters" in the language of the Native American Sho-Ban tribe. So he went with that.

The Comeback Trail

Street never gave up after her crash. Three months later, she joined the US Ski Team for a World Cup stop in Japan. This was her one chance to see

Rosi Mittermaier

West German Rosi Mittermaier began skiing on the World Cup circuit at 16 in 1966, its first season. Over the next 10 years, she never won a downhill race in the World Cup. Yet Mittermaier claimed her first gold at the 1976 Olympics in Innsbruck, Austria. Three days later, she won the slalom. And two days after that, she nearly won a third gold medal. Mittermaier won a silver medal in the giant slalom. She missed gold by 12-hundredths of a second. A win would have made her the first woman to win three Alpine gold medals in one Olympics. She retired three months later at 25.

the Olympic course up close. She convinced US downhill assistant coach Andreas Rickenbach to give her a piggyback ride down the hill.

By fall, Street was training at the Copper Mountain ski resort in Colorado. She was on the chairlift at 6:15 a.m. Her coaches had to set up the course in the dark. The ski patrol rode snowmobiles with headlights on to help them see.

By December 17, Street was back skiing on the World Cup circuit. She finished tenth in a downhill at Val d'Isere, France. A day later, she was eleventh in a super-G. Races in Austria and Italy followed. Then she went to Sweden for a downhill on January 31. The Olympics began in Nagano just eight days later. However, Street crashed during her run. She was

Hanni Wenzel

Hanni Wenzel was born in 1956 in Straubing, West Germany. One year later, her family moved to Liechtenstein. At the time, the country in Central Europe had a population of approximately 25,000. In 1974, Wenzel won the slalom at the World Championships. She was also granted citizenship. Two years later, she won a bronze medal in the slalom at the 1976 Olympics. It was the first medal for the tiny country. In 1980, she won the slalom and giant slalom, and was second in the downhill. Her gold medals were the only ones won by Liechtenstein in any sport. However, two days before she won her first gold, her brother, Andreas, took silver in the men's giant slalom.

knocked unconscious. And she remained that way for two minutes. It was her second horrific crash in 13 months. Yet she remained determined.

Street was entered in both the super-G and downhill at the Olympics. Super-G was first. But it was Street's weaker event. She had never won a super-G on the World Cup circuit. Then she drew the No. 2 starting position. Skiers usually prefer later starts so they know what they have to beat. Few thought much of her chances.

Street, on the other hand, saw an opportunity. She noted that the course was set up more like a downhill than a super-G. There were not as many gates. Plus, it was relatively straight. So she decided to use her

US skiers carry teammate Picabo Street in celebration after she won the 1998 Olympic gold medal in the super-G.

downhill skis. They are about 4 inches (10 cm) longer than super-G skis. That makes them faster but harder to turn.

She started quickly. She had a bobble in midrace but overcame it and finished with a time of 1 minute, 18.02 seconds. Now came the waiting game. Street had to watch as everybody else tried to beat her time.

Alexandra Meissnitzer of Austria skied three spots behind Street. She gave Street a scare. But the Austrian finished seven-hundredths of a second behind. Fellow Austrian Michaela Dorfmeister went down eighteenth. She made Street's heart stop. She matched Street at every intermediate timing point down the course. Only one time mattered, though. Dorfmeister finished one-hundredth of a second behind Street at 1:18.03.

Fellow Germans Seizinger and Hilde Gerg were also favorites. So was Switzerland's Heidi Zurbriggen. But none of them came close. Street fulfilled her promise to win a gold medal.

The accomplishment struck her later that night. Street, who also finished sixth in the downhill in Nagano, was standing on the top step of the podium when she received her gold medal. Fighting back tears, she sang "The Star-Spangled Banner." She sang loudly and off key, but she didn't care. She was an Olympic champion.

Nikki Stone

Nikki Stone had an up-and-down road to a medal. The US aerials skier was a favorite to medal at the 1994 Olympics. Instead, she didn't make it out of the qualifying round. One year later Stone claimed the world championship and the World Cup title. But soon after that, a chronic back injury prevented her from standing. She couldn't ski for nine months. But Stone persevered. During the 1997–98 season, she won four of six events. Her big moment came at the 1998 Olympics. Her two major rivals, Kirstie Marshall and Jacqui Cooper of Australia, were eliminated in qualifying. Despite gusting winds, which are dangerous in aerial skiing, Stone was the only one to attempt a triple somersault. She landed the jump on her second attempt and won handily.

6

Vancouver 2010
NEW DAY
IN NORDIC

Billy Demong and his US Nordic combined skiing teammates were used to disappointment. The 2002 Olympic Winter Games were in Salt Lake City, Utah. There, the US team finished fourth in the team relay, just short of winning Team USA's first medal in Nordic combined.

Later that year, Demong was horsing around with his friends at a pool. He dived into the shallow end and struck his head on the bottom. He was lucky. That could

Team USA's Johnny Spillane, *left*, and Billy Demong complete the transition in the team event at the 2010 Olympic Winter Games in Vancouver, Canada.

have paralyzed him. Demong suffered only a fractured skull. But it kept him out of competition for a year.

The disappointment continued in 2009. Nordic combined competitions begin with a ski jump. The result in ski jump determines the order in which athletes start in a cross-country ski race. Skiers race 10 kilometers in individual events. In the team relay, four athletes per team each race five kilometers. At that year's World Championships, Demong lost his bib before the ski jumping part of the team event. And because of that, the US team was disqualified. He later discovered the bib had slipped down his ski suit. He found it in his boot.

Bill Koch

Not a single US reporter was on hand at the 30-kilometer cross-country race at the 1976 Olympics. They figured no American had a shot at medaling. After all, no US Nordic skier had medaled at the Winter Games since Norwegian-born Anders Haugen took a ski jumping bronze medal in 1924. And Haugen was only awarded his medal 50 years later when someone noticed a scoring error. Then Billy Koch stunned the world in 1976. The self-described loner raced to second place. His time of one hour, 30 minutes, 57.84 seconds, was nearly half a minute behind Sergei Savelyev of the Soviet Union. But it was more than 10 seconds ahead of another Soviet, bronze medalist Ivan Garanin. Koch later introduced what has become known as the skating technique in competitive cross-country skiing.

There had been successes along the way. His teammate Johnny Spillane had won a world title in 2003. That made him the first American to win a major trophy in Nordic combined. Demong won an individual medal at the 2009 World Championships. That was the same event where he lost his bib. But Nordic combined had been an Olympic event since the first Winter Games in 1924. And the United States had never won an Olympic medal. Demong and his teammates were eager to change that at the 2010 Olympics in Vancouver, Canada.

Their quest began in the normal hill event. That is the smaller of the two ski jump hills. There, Spillane broke through to win a silver medal. Fellow American Todd Lodwick finished two spots behind him. Demong was sixth. Nine days later, the United States followed that up with another silver medal, this time in the team relay.

But that, too, had its disappointment. Team USA had led after the first two legs of the relay. But it lost the lead on the third five-kilometer lap, skied by Spillane. Demong skied the final five kilometers. He retook the lead. But he couldn't hold off Mario Stecher. The Austrian passed Demong in the stretch to win the gold.

Now only one event remained. The individual large hill event was the Americans' last chance for a gold medal. Demong wasn't going to waste it.

American Todd Lodwick competes in ski jump during the individual normal hill competition at the 2010 Olympics.

Billy's Ride

Two-thirds of the ski jumpers had already competed when the wind changed. Officials decided to restart the event. When it finally finished, Austria's Bernhard Gruber led. That meant he would begin the 10-kilometer cross-country race in the front. Spillane had finished second and started 34 seconds back. Demong was sixth. He had to start 46 seconds behind Gruber and 12 seconds behind Spillane.

Demong started quickly. He joined Spillane within the first kilometer. The two began to chase Gruber. They caught the Austrian near the race's midpoint. From there, the three skied together in a three-man group.

Lodwick, meanwhile, started the cross-country race in thirteenth place. He was 73 seconds behind Gruber. But Lodwick had climbed into fourth by the midway point. He was ahead of the main group of skiers. Lodwick saw his teammates ahead and had a choice to make. He was in position to keep pushing forward and try for his own Olympic medal. Or he could stay back and help his teammates win by limiting the chase group. He was competing in his fifth Olympics. It was his fourth with both Demong and Spillane. All three had been part of the team that just missed out on the medal in 2002. He chose loyalty.

Bjorn Daehlie

At age 20, Bjorn Daehlie traveled to the 1988 Olympics as a member of the Norwegian Nordic ski team. However, he didn't compete in a single race in Calgary, Canada. Four years later, Daehlie won three gold medals in Albertville, France. They were in the combined pursuit and blue-ribbon 50-kilometer individual events and the 40-kilometer team relay. He also won silver in the 30-kilometer race. It was the beginning of a career that would result in him becoming the second-most decorated Winter Olympian with 12 medals, eight of them gold.

Billy Demong crosses the finish line to win the gold medal
in the individual large hill event at the 2010
Olympic Winter Games.

"Once I saw those two guys pull away, I jumped in front [of the chase group] and tried to slow down the pace," Lodwick said.

By the start of the final kilometer, Demong had pulled away from Gruber, who had moved into second. Spillane had dropped to third. Gruber faded in the final 500 meters while Demong pushed to the finish. He won with a time of 25:32.9. Then Spillane passed Gruber and claimed the silver medal. He was four seconds behind Demong. The result gave the United States its first two individual Olympic medals in Nordic combined. Demong's gold was Team USA's first in the sport. Gruber ended up 10.8 seconds back in third. Lodwick, meanwhile, faded to thirteenth. He was 70 seconds behind Demong.

"Having gone through all of these things has made this [success] that much sweeter," Demong said.

It wasn't the end of the perfect day, though. Later that night while celebrating at the US Ski Team's headquarters, Demong proposed to his girlfriend, Katie Koczynski. While he was down on one knee, he got another surprise. Officials notified Demong that he had been selected to carry the US flag at the Closing Ceremony of the Olympics. All of his disappointment and heartbreak were just a distant memory.

Sochi 2014
A NEW ERA

The 2014 Winter Olympics in Sochi, Russia, were only a few days away. Yet US freeskier Joss Christensen wasn't even sure he was going. Christensen is a slopestyle skier. His event was one of four new freestyle skiing events making their Olympic debut in 2014. For Christensen, just getting on the plane would be enough of a victory.

It had been a tough six months for Christensen. His dad, J. D., had died the previous August from a heart condition. J. D. had been Joss's biggest fan. Christensen

Joss Christensen performs a trick during the slopestyle qualification rounds at the 2014 Olympic Winter Games in Sochi, Russia.

was on a plane to New Zealand for preseason training when his father died.

The skier's performances suffered. He was thirty-sixth in the World Cup standings when the season took a break for the Olympics. That was the sixth-best standing among the Americans. Only four US slopestyle skiers would be selected to compete in Sochi. Ten days before the event, however, officials named Christensen as one of the lucky four. That was pretty much Christensen's gold medal.

The Olympics got off to a good start for Christensen. He carried a photo of his dad as he marched with Team USA in the Opening Ceremony. His spirits remained high when he took the hill for slopestyle qualifying. And to the surprise of many, Christensen was awarded the two best scores of the round. All three of his US teammates—Nick Goepper, Gus Kenworthy, and Bobby Brown—moved on to the final round, too.

Making History

The result gave Christensen a lot of confidence. Slopestyle has several elements to it. The skiers start at the top of a large terrain park. On the way down, skiers slide on rails and boxes. There are also three massive jumps. Each competitor gets two attempts to impress five judges. The judges rate the skier from 0 to 100 based on six elements: execution of their tricks, how high they get on the jumps, variety, perceived difficulty, artistry of the run's progression, and specific combination of tricks. The high and the low scores are discarded and the other three are averaged. Each skier has two runs per round. Only the higher score counts in the final standings.

Twelve skiers advanced to the final round. As the top qualifier, Christensen skied last. The score to beat going into his first run was Goepper's 92.40. Christensen had scored better than that in qualifying. He felt good about his chances.

The rails and boxes at the top of the course went as planned. His first jump was a perfectly executed double cork 1260 with a double Japan

Mikaela Shiffrin

Two days before the 2014 Olympic slalom, American Mikaela Shiffrin came down with a cold. It barely slowed her down. She led by 49-hundredths of a second after her first run. That meant she would ski last in her second run. Shiffrin's idol, 32-year-old Marlies Schild of Austria, was leading when Shiffrin began her final run. But Schild had been 1.34 seconds slower than Shiffrin in the first run. That meant the US skier only had to beat Schild's time by 1.34 seconds. Shiffrin nearly fell halfway down. But she kept her skis moving. And when she crossed the finish line, Shiffrin was 53-hundreths ahead. At 18, she became the youngest Olympic slalom champion ever.

grab. That is a double backward somersault, rotating three and a half times while grabbing his opposite skis behind the binding. His second jump was a switch right-side double cork 1080 with a tail grab. He took off backward, spun to his right, and rotated three times. All the while he somersaulted twice and grabbed the back of one of his skis.

After landing that, Christensen tried something he learned only days before. His last jump was a switch triple cork 1260 with a Japan grab. Taking off backward, he twirled three and a half times, somersaulted three times, and grabbed one of his skis. Christensen nailed all three jumps. The judges gave him a 95.80. He was 3.40 points ahead of Goepper. Andreas Haatveit of Norway was in third with 89.60.

Ted Ligety

Ted Ligety already had won an Olympic gold medal in the combined in 2006. But his best event was the giant slalom. The American had won four World Cup giant slalom crowns and two world championships in the event by the time he arrived at the 2014 Olympics. But he missed a medal in the event at the 2010 Olympics. Ligety felt he skied too conservatively. So he wanted to be aggressive in 2014. And he was. Ligety led by 93-hundredths of a second after the first run. It was enough that he only had to have the fourteenth-best time in the second run. And he still won by nearly half of a second. Ligety became the first US man (and only the second American) to win two Olympic gold medals in Alpine skiing. He was the first US man to win the Olympic giant slalom.

US slopestyle skiers, *from left*, Gus Kenworthy, Joss Christensen, and Nick Goepper celebrate a medal sweep at the 2014 Olympic Winter Games.

Christensen was again set to go last in the second run. He waited as the first 11 skiers went. Of the first nine, only Kenworthy scored in the 90s. He moved into second with a score of 93.60. Goepper fell to third. Then Haatveit scored 91.80 on his second try. That meant he would not make the medal podium. US skiers were assured of winning gold, silver, and bronze. It was only the third time in Winter Olympics history that the United States had swept the medals in an event.

Goepper still had an opportunity to move up to second or first. But he flubbed his last run and scored 61.80. That meant Christensen had won without even having to take his final run. He still went for it, though. And with nothing to lose or gain, he scored 93.80. That was the second highest score of the day.

Bright Future

Freestyle skiing had been rising in popularity since its Olympic debut in 1992. Yet 2014 proved to be a milestone year. Halfpipe, slopestyle, and skicross joined aerials and moguls in the Olympic program. And Team USA won seven medals in the freestyle events. That represented a quarter of the total medals Team USA won in all sports in 2014.

Besides Christensen, Maddie Bowman and David Wise won the women's and men's halfpipe, respectively. Devin Logan claimed silver in the women's slopestyle. Hannah Kearney, who won gold in 2010 in women's moguls, added a bronze to her collection. For Team USA, it was a strong start to a new generation of Olympic skiing.

Great Olympians

Kjetil Andre Aamodt (Norway)

The Alpine skier won eight Olympic medals from 1992 to 2006, making him the most decorated Alpine skier. He is the only man with four Alpine gold medals.

Bjorn Daehlie (Norway)

The cross-country skier won 12 medals from 1992 to 1998, including eight gold medals. Only countryman and biathlete Ole Einar Bjorndalen has won more Winter Olympic medals through 2014.

Jean-Claude Killy (France)

Killy won the downhill, slalom, and giant slalom in 1968, one of only two men to sweep all three events at one Olympics.

Janica Kostelic (Croatia)

Kostelic is the only woman to have won four gold medals in Alpine skiing at the Olympics, which she did from 1998 to 2006. Her older brother, Ivica Kostelic, won four Olympic silver medals.

Andrea Mead-Lawrence (USA)

The only US woman to win two gold medals in skiing at the Olympics, she won both the slalom and giant slalom in 1952 at 19.

Bode Miller (USA)

The most decorated US Alpine skier at the Olympics, Miller won his sixth medal at the 2014 Games. It was his fifth Olympics. Miller won his sole gold medal in the combined in 2010.

Matti Nykanen (Finland)

Nykanen is the most successful Olympic ski jumper in history with five medals, including four gold, from 1984 to 1988. He was the first to win both the large and normal hills events at the same Olympics.

Raisa Smetanina (Soviet Union)

From 1976 to 1992, the cross-country skier won the most medals by a woman (10: four gold, five silver, one bronze) at the Winter Games.

Glossary

BINDING

A device that attaches a boot to a ski. Alpine ski boots connect on the front and back, while Nordic boots only connect at the front.

EDGE

Small strips of metal or other material that are attached to skis to give them more grip in the snow.

GATE

A marker, usually a pole or poles with a flag on top, that defines a course and that an Alpine skier must go around or between.

HALFPIPE

An event in which skiers perform tricks on a U-shaped run. Similar to slopestyle, each skier gets two runs with only the better score counting.

INTERMEDIATE MARK

An unofficial checkpoint that tells an athlete's time midway through a race.

LEGS

Portions of a relay race. Each athlete competes in one leg.

MOGULS

A small mound or knoll on a downhill slope that skiers must go over or around. Competitive mogul skiing requires a skier to get down a hill covered by moguls and twice perform tricks off a ramp.

NORDIC COMBINED

A sport that combines the Nordic disciplines of ski jumping and cross-country skiing. Skiers first compete in ski jumping. Those with the best jumps get a head start in a cross-country race.

RACE JURY

A group of officials who review protests and accusations of rules violations for a race.

SKICROSS

A downhill ski race in which the athletes compete against each other, rather than against the clock. They must go over various jumps and other obstacles on the way down.

For More
Information

SELECTED BIBLIOGRAPHY

Boswell, Thomas. "By Whatever Name, Tomba Stamps the Olympics." *The Washington Post*. Cengage Learning, 26 Feb. 1988. Web. 24 Feb. 2014.

Donaldson, Amy. "2010 Winter Olympics: After Suffering Disappointment, Injury, American Billy Demong Wins Gold." *Deseret News*. Deseret News, 26 Feb. 2010. Web. 24 Feb. 2014.

Wallechinsky, David, and Jaime Loucky. *The Complete Book of the Winter Olympics: 2010 Edition*. London, UK: Aurum Press, 2009.

Wukovits, John. *The Encyclopedia of the Winter Olympics*. New York: Franklin Watts, 2001.

FURTHER READINGS

Burns, Kylie. *Alpine and Freestyle Skiing*. New York: Crabtree Pub. Co., 2009.

Burns, Kylie. *Biathlon, Cross-Country, Ski Jumping, and Nordic Combined*. New York: Crabtree Pub. Co., 2010.

Hunter, Nick. *The Winter Olympics*. London, UK: Heinemann, 2013.

Richardson, Kyle. *Unofficial Olympic Guidebook: Freestyle Skiing*. Vacaville, CA: PYP Publishing, 2013.

WEBSITES

To learn more about Great Moments in Olympic Sports, visit **booklinks.abdopublishing.com**. These links are routinely monitored and updated to provide the most current information available.

PLACES TO VISIT

The Ski Museum
Kongeveien 5
0787 Oslo
Norway
+47 916 71 947
www.holmenkollen.com/eng/The-Ski-Museum
The world's oldest museum dedicated to ski history. Among the exhibits is a rock carving of a cave man skiing that is approximately 4,000 years old and skis that date back to 600 CE.

US Ski and Snowboard Hall of Fame and Museum
610 Palms Ave.
Ishpeming, MI 49849
(906) 485-6323
www.skihall.com
The birthplace of organized skiing in the United States. It contains displays and exhibits with countless artifacts relating to the history of skiing and snowboarding.

Index

ABOUT THE AUTHOR

Brian Trusdell has been a sportswriter for more than 30 years with The Associated Press and Bloomberg News. He has reported from six Olympics, including the Winter Games of 1994 in Lillehammer, Norway, and 1998 in Nagano, Japan. He also has covered four FIFA World Cups and has traveled to every continent except Antarctica. He lives in New Jersey with his wife.